filled with gratitude

My Personal info

- ♥ Name
- ♥ Address
- ♥ Phone
- ♥ Facebook
- ♥ Instagram
- ♥ E-Mail

·2021·

wake up and be fabulous wake up and be fabulous

Calendar
2021

01
JANUARY

Su	Mo	Tu	We	Th	Fr	Sa
					1	2
3	4	5	6	7	8	9
10	11	12	13	14	15	16
17	18	19	20	21	22	23
24	25	26	27	28	29	30
31						

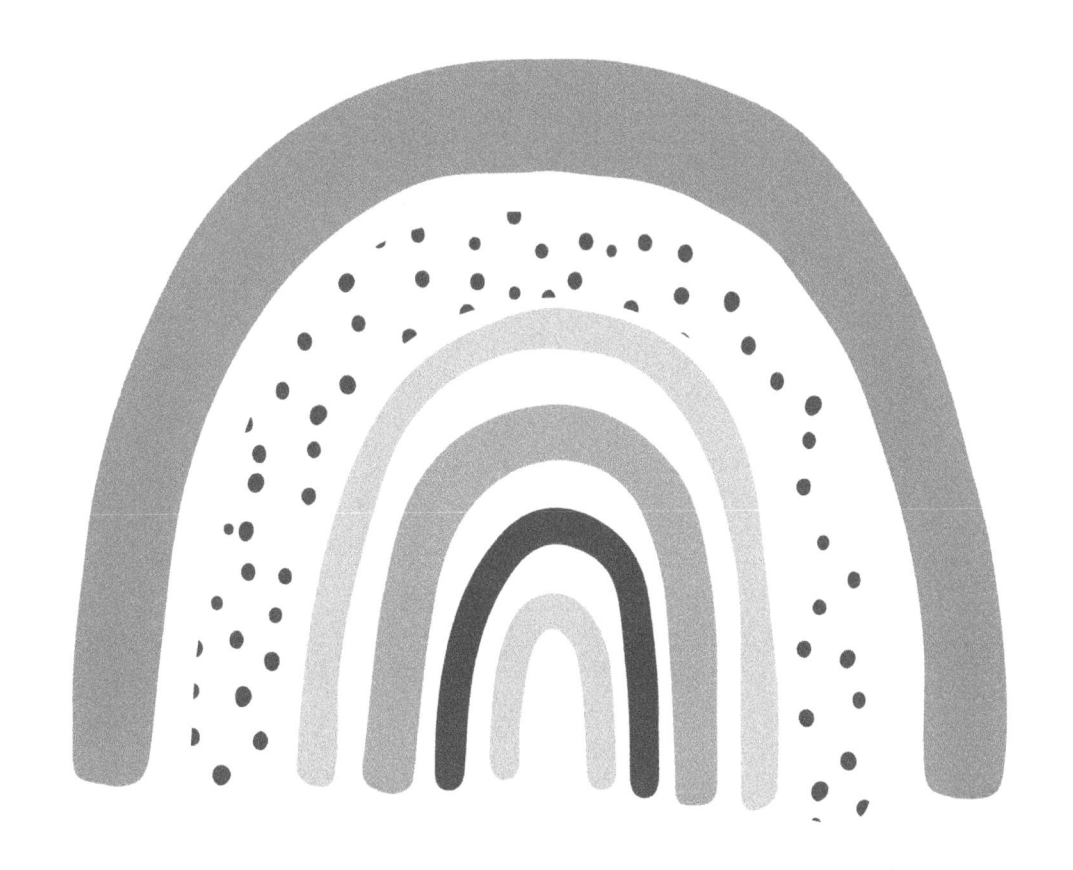

02

FEBRUARY

Su	Mo	Tu	We	Th	Fr	Sa
	1	2	3	4	5	6
7	8	9	10	11	12	13
14	15	16	17	18	19	20
21	22	23	24	25	26	27
28						

03
MARCH

Su	Mo	Tu	We	Th	Fr	Sa
	1	2	3	4	5	6
7	8	9	10	11	12	13
14	15	16	17	18	19	20
21	22	23	24	25	26	27
28	29	30	31			

04
APRIL

Su	Mo	Tu	We	Th	Fr	Sa
				1	2	3
4	5	6	7	8	9	10
11	12	13	14	15	16	17
18	19	20	21	22	23	24
25	26	27	28	29	30	

05
MAY

Su	Mo	Tu	We	Th	Fr	Sa
						1
2	3	4	5	6	7	8
9	10	11	12	13	14	15
16	17	18	19	20	21	22
23	24	25	26	27	28	29
30	31					

06
JUNE

Su	Mo	Tu	We	Th	Fr	Sa
		1	2	3	4	5
6	7	8	9	10	11	12
13	14	15	16	17	18	19
20	21	22	23	24	25	26
27	28	29	30			

07
JULY

Su	Mo	Tu	We	Th	Fr	Sa
				1	2	3
4	5	6	7	8	9	10
11	12	13	14	15	16	17
18	19	20	21	22	23	24
25	26	27	28	29	30	31

08
AUGUST

Su	Mo	Tu	We	Th	Fr	Sa
1	2	3	4	5	6	7
8	9	10	11	12	13	14
15	16	17	18	19	20	21
22	23	24	25	26	27	28
29	30	31				

09
SEPTEMBER

Su	Mo	Tu	We	Th	Fr	Sa
			1	2	3	4
5	6	7	8	9	10	11
12	13	14	15	16	17	18
19	20	21	22	23	24	25
26	27	28	29	30		

10
OCTOBER

Su	Mo	Tu	We	Th	Fr	Sa
					1	2
3	4	5	6	7	8	9
10	11	12	13	14	15	16
17	18	19	20	21	22	23
24	25	26	27	28	29	30
31						

11

NOVEMBER

Su	Mo	Tu	We	Th	Fr	Sa
	1	2	3	4	5	6
7	8	9	10	11	12	13
14	15	16	17	18	19	20
21	22	23	24	25	26	27
28	29	30				

12

DECEMBER

Su	Mo	Tu	We	Th	Fr	Sa
			1	2	3	4
5	6	7	8	9	10	11
12	13	14	15	16	17	18
19	20	21	22	23	24	25
26	27	28	29	30	31	

MINDFULNESS DAILY JOURNAL

Date: _____/_____/20___

Sun ○ Mon ○ Tue ○ Wed ○ Thu ○ Fri ○ Sat ○

IDEAS

MY MOOD TODAY

😊 ☹️ 😦 😄 😠

Today Will Be A Good Day

Meditation

How long? _____/_____   How was it?   Hard ○   Easy ○

Excercise ○   Yoga/Walking/Gym/Other _____

Today I Choose to Feel
_____
_____
_____

Today I Will Focus on
_____
_____
_____

Today I feel Inspired By
_____
_____
_____

Good Habits of The Day
_____
_____
_____

To Do List
- ○ _____
- ○ _____
- ○ _____
- ○ _____
- ○ _____
- ○ _____

Today I'm Grateful for

GRATITUDE

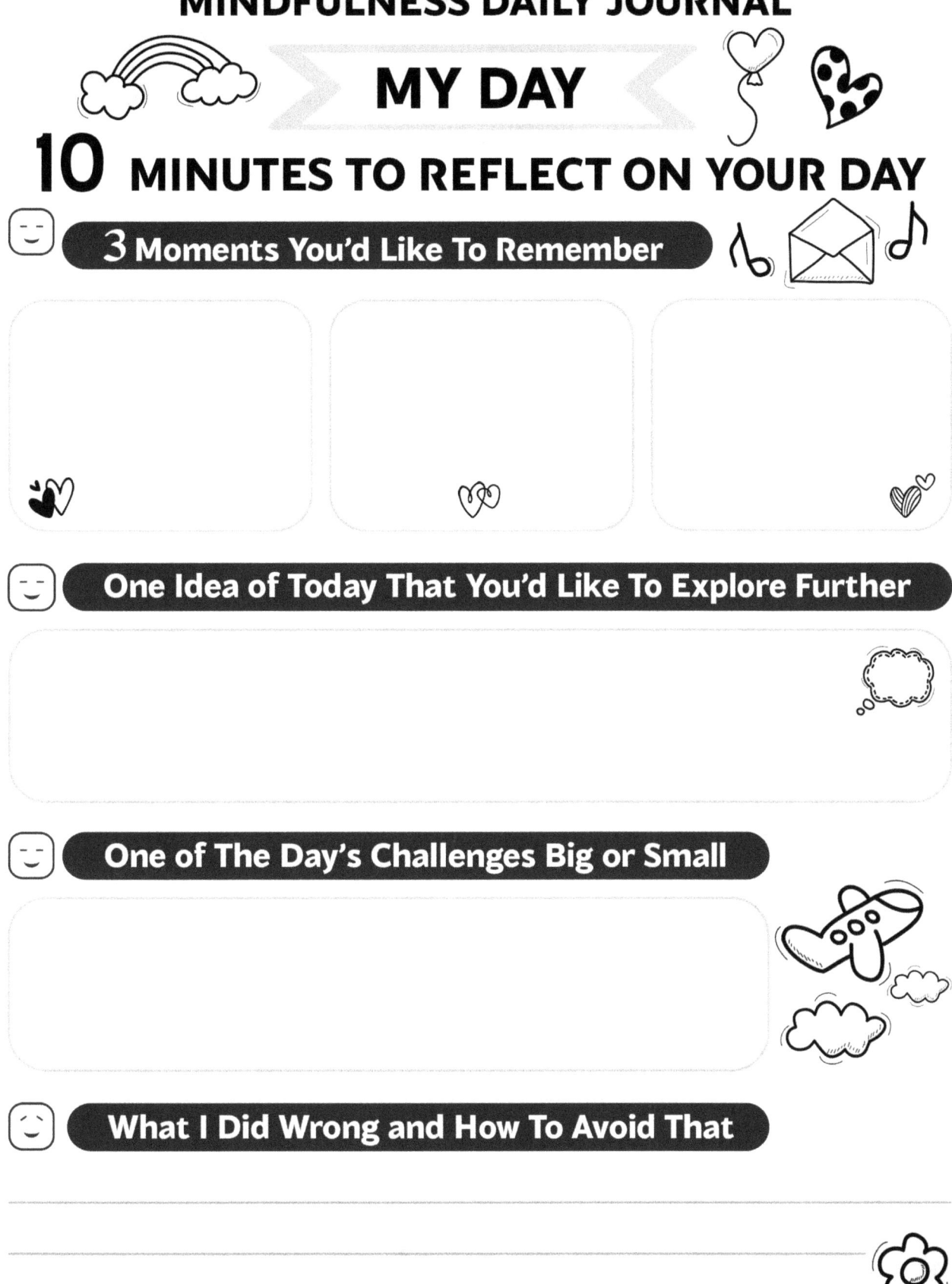

MINDFULNESS DAILY JOURNAL

MY DAY

10 MINUTES TO REFLECT ON YOUR DAY

3 Moments You'd Like To Remember

One Idea of Today That You'd Like To Explore Further

One of The Day's Challenges Big or Small

What I Did Wrong and How To Avoid That

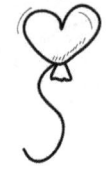

MINDFULNESS DAILY JOURNAL

JOURNAL

goal

MINDFULNESS DAILY JOURNAL

Date: _____/_____/20__

Sun ○ Mon ○ Tue ○ Wed ○ Thu ○ Fri ○ Sat ○

IDEAS

MY MOOD TODAY

🙂 ☹ 😐 😄 😮

Today Will Be A Good Day

Meditation

How long? _____ / _____

How was it? Hard ○ Easy ○

Excercise ○   Yoga/Walking/Gym/Other _____

Today I Choose to Feel
_____
_____
_____

Today I Will Focus on
_____
_____
_____

Today I feel Inspired By
_____
_____
_____

Good Habits of The Day
_____
_____
_____

To Do List
- _____
- _____
- _____
- _____
- _____

Today I'm Grateful for
_____
_____
_____
_____
_____

MINDFULNESS DAILY JOURNAL

MY DAY

10 MINUTES TO REFLECT ON YOUR DAY

3 Moments You'd Like To Remember

One Idea of Today That You'd Like To Explore Further

One of The Day's Challenges Big or Small

What I Did Wrong and How To Avoid That

MINDFULNESS DAILY JOURNAL

JOURNAL

goal

MINDFULNESS DAILY JOURNAL

Date: _____/_____/20__

Sun ○ Mon ○ Tue ○ Wed ○ Thu ○ Fri ○ Sat ○

IDEAS

MY MOOD TODAY

Today Will Be A Good Day

Meditation

How long? _____ /_____   How was it?   Hard ○   Easy ○

Excercise ○   Yoga/Walking/Gym/Other _____

Today I Choose to Feel

_____
_____
_____

Today I Will Focus on

_____
_____
_____

Today I feel Inspired By

_____
_____
_____

Good Habits of The Day

_____
_____
_____

To Do List

○ _____
○ _____
○ _____
○ _____
○ _____
○ _____

Today I'm Grateful for

MINDFULNESS DAILY JOURNAL

MY DAY

10 MINUTES TO REFLECT ON YOUR DAY

3 Moments You'd Like To Remember

One Idea of Today That You'd Like To Explore Further

One of The Day's Challenges Big or Small

What I Did Wrong and How To Avoid That

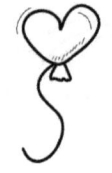

MINDFULNESS DAILY JOURNAL

JOURNAL

goal

MINDFULNESS DAILY JOURNAL

Date: _____/_____/20__

Sun ◯ Mon ◯ Tue ◯ Wed ◯ Thu ◯ Fri ◯ Sat ◯

IDEAS

MY MOOD TODAY

🙂 🙁 😟 😄 😠

Today Will Be A Good Day

Meditation

How long? _____ /_____   How was it?   Hard ◯   Easy ◯

Excercise ◯   Yoga/Walking/Gym/Other _____

Today I Choose to Feel

_____
_____
_____

Today I Will Focus on

_____
_____
_____

Today I feel Inspired By

_____
_____
_____

Good Habits of The Day

_____
_____
_____

To Do List

◯ _____
◯ _____
◯ _____
◯ _____
◯ _____
◯ _____

Today I'm Grateful for

MINDFULNESS DAILY JOURNAL

MY DAY

10 MINUTES TO REFLECT ON YOUR DAY

3 Moments You'd Like To Remember

One Idea of Today That You'd Like To Explore Further

One of The Day's Challenges Big or Small

What I Did Wrong and How To Avoid That

MINDFULNESS DAILY JOURNAL

JOURNAL

goal

MINDFULNESS DAILY JOURNAL

Date: _____/_____/20__

Sun Mon Tue Wed Thu Fri Sat

IDEAS

MY MOOD TODAY

Today will be a Good Day

Meditation

How long? _____/_____

How was it?   Hard ○   Easy ○

Excercise ○   Yoga/Walking/Gym/Other _____

Today I Choose to Feel

Today I Will Focus on

Today I feel Inspired By

Good Habits of The Day

To Do List

Today I'm Grateful for

MINDFULNESS DAILY JOURNAL

MY DAY

10 MINUTES TO REFLECT ON YOUR DAY

3 Moments You'd Like To Remember

One Idea of Today That You'd Like To Explore Further

One of The Day's Challenges Big or Small

What I Did Wrong and How To Avoid That

MINDFULNESS DAILY JOURNAL

JOURNAL

goal

MINDFULNESS DAILY JOURNAL

Date: _____/_____/20__

Sun ◯ Mon ◯ Tue ◯ Wed ◯ Thu ◯ Fri ◯ Sat ◯

IDEAS

MY MOOD TODAY
😊 ☹ 😐 😄 😠

Today Will Be A Good Day

Meditation

How long? _____/_____   How was it? Hard ◯ Easy ◯

Excercise ◯   Yoga/Walking/Gym/Other _____

Today I Choose to Feel
_____
_____
_____

Today I Will Focus on
_____
_____
_____

Today I feel Inspired By
_____
_____
_____

Good Habits of The Day
_____
_____
_____

To Do List
_____
_____
_____
_____
_____

Today I'm Grateful for

MINDFULNESS DAILY JOURNAL

MY DAY

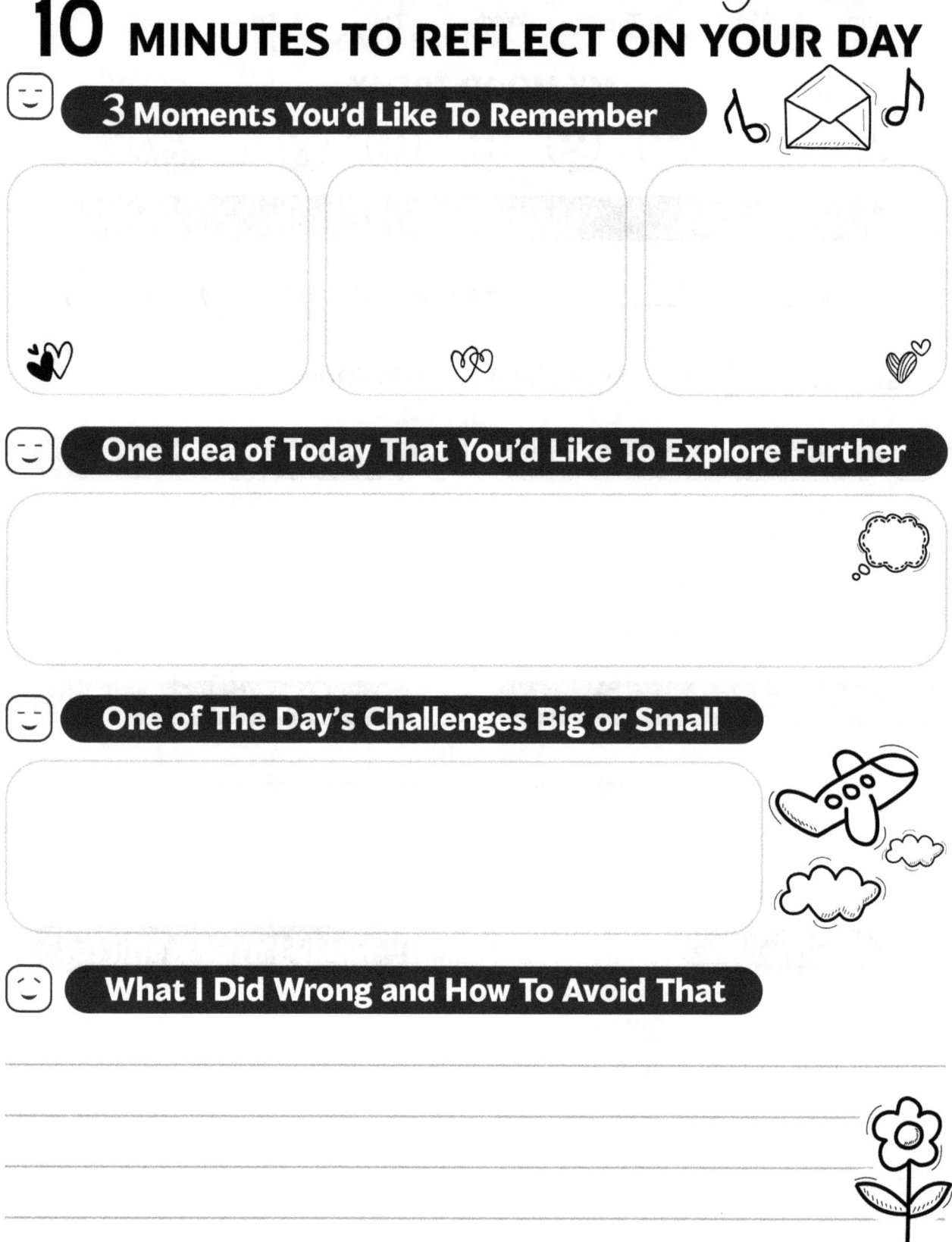

10 MINUTES TO REFLECT ON YOUR DAY

3 Moments You'd Like To Remember

One Idea of Today That You'd Like To Explore Further

One of The Day's Challenges Big or Small

What I Did Wrong and How To Avoid That

MINDFULNESS DAILY JOURNAL

JOURNAL

goal

MINDFULNESS DAILY JOURNAL

Date: _____/_____/20__

Sun ○ Mon ○ Tue ○ Wed ○ Thu ○ Fri ○ Sat ○

IDEAS

MY MOOD TODAY
☺ ☹ ☹ 😄 😠

Today Will Be A Good Day

Meditation

How long? _____/_____   How was it? Hard ○   Easy ○

Excercise ○   Yoga/Walking/Gym/Other _____

Today I Choose to Feel

Today I Will Focus on

Today I feel Inspired By

Good Habits of The Day

To Do List

Today I'm Grateful for

MINDFULNESS DAILY JOURNAL

MY DAY

10 MINUTES TO REFLECT ON YOUR DAY

3 Moments You'd Like To Remember

One Idea of Today That You'd Like To Explore Further

One of The Day's Challenges Big or Small

What I Did Wrong and How To Avoid That

MINDFULNESS DAILY JOURNAL

JOURNAL

goal

MINDFULNESS DAILY JOURNAL

Date: _____/_____/20__

Sun ○ Mon ○ Tue ○ Wed ○ Thu ○ Fri ○ Sat ○

IDEAS

MY MOOD TODAY

Today Will Be A Good Day

Meditation

How long? _____/_____   How was it? Hard ○ Easy ○

Excercise ○   Yoga/Walking/Gym/Other _____

Today I Choose to Feel

_____
_____
_____

Today I Will Focus on

_____
_____
_____

Today I feel Inspired By

_____
_____
_____

Good Habits of The Day

_____
_____
_____

To Do List

○ _____
○ _____
○ _____
○ _____
○ _____
○ _____

Today I'm Grateful for

MINDFULNESS DAILY JOURNAL

MY DAY

10 MINUTES TO REFLECT ON YOUR DAY

3 Moments You'd Like To Remember

One Idea of Today That You'd Like To Explore Further

One of The Day's Challenges Big or Small

What I Did Wrong and How To Avoid That

MINDFULNESS DAILY JOURNAL

JOURNAL

goal

MINDFULNESS DAILY JOURNAL

Date: _____/_____/20___

Sun ○ Mon ○ Tue ○ Wed ○ Thu ○ Fri ○ Sat ○

IDEAS

MY MOOD TODAY

😊 😕 ☹️ 😄 😠

Today Will Be A Good Day

Meditation

How long? _____ / _____

How was it? Hard ○ Easy ○

Excercise ○   Yoga/Walking/Gym/Other _____

Today I Choose to Feel
_____
_____
_____

Today I Will Focus on
_____
_____
_____

Today I feel Inspired By
_____
_____
_____

Good Habits of The Day
_____
_____
_____

To Do List
○ _____
○ _____
○ _____
○ _____
○ _____
○ _____

Today I'm Grateful for

MINDFULNESS DAILY JOURNAL

MY DAY

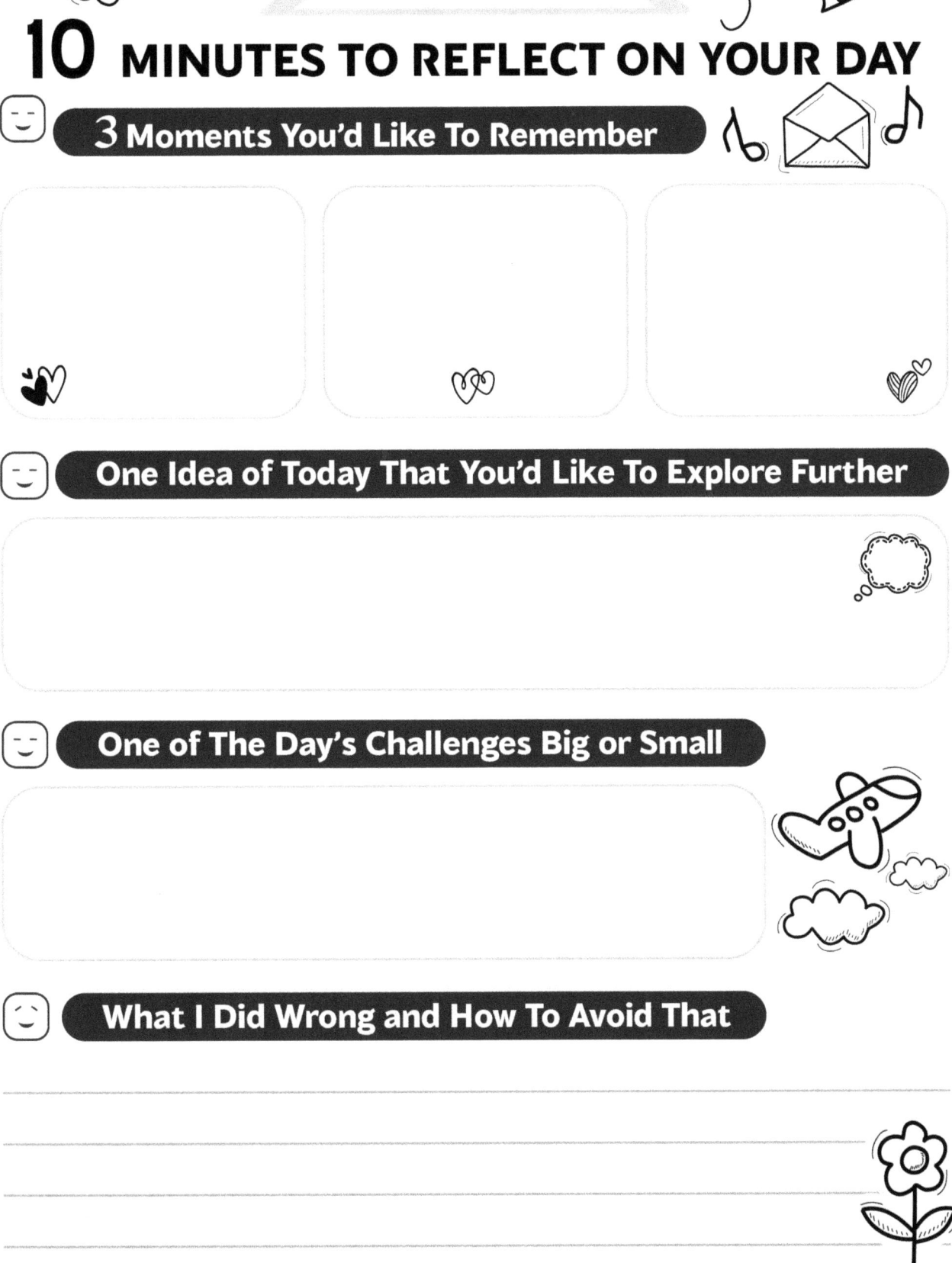

10 MINUTES TO REFLECT ON YOUR DAY

3 Moments You'd Like To Remember

One Idea of Today That You'd Like To Explore Further

One of The Day's Challenges Big or Small

What I Did Wrong and How To Avoid That

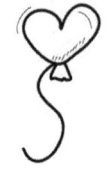

MINDFULNESS DAILY JOURNAL

JOURNAL

goal

MINDFULNESS DAILY JOURNAL

Date: _____/_____/20__

Sun ◯ Mon ◯ Tue ◯ Wed ◯ Thu ◯ Fri ◯ Sat ◯

IDEAS

MY MOOD TODAY

Today Will Be A Good Day

Meditation

How long? _____/_____   How was it? Hard ◯ Easy ◯

Excercise ◯   Yoga/Walking/Gym/Other _____

Today I Choose to Feel

_____
_____
_____

Today I Will Focus on

_____
_____
_____

Today I feel Inspired By

_____
_____
_____

Good Habits of The Day

_____
_____
_____

To Do List

◯ _____
◯ _____
◯ _____
◯ _____
◯ _____
◯ _____

Today I'm Grateful for

_____
_____
_____
_____

MINDFULNESS DAILY JOURNAL

MY DAY

10 MINUTES TO REFLECT ON YOUR DAY

3 Moments You'd Like To Remember

One Idea of Today That You'd Like To Explore Further

One of The Day's Challenges Big or Small

What I Did Wrong and How To Avoid That

MINDFULNESS DAILY JOURNAL

JOURNAL

goal

MINDFULNESS DAILY JOURNAL

Date: _____ /_____ /20__

Sun ○ Mon ○ Tue ○ Wed ○ Thu ○ Fri ○ Sat ○

IDEAS

MY MOOD TODAY

🙂 ☹️ 😦 😄 😠

Today will be a Good Day

Meditation

How long? _____ / _____   How was it? Hard ○ Easy ○

Excercise ○   Yoga/Walking/Gym/Other _____

Today I Choose to Feel
_____
_____
_____

Today I Will Focus on
_____
_____
_____

Today I feel Inspired By
_____
_____
_____

Good Habits of The Day
_____
_____
_____

To Do List
○ _____
○ _____
○ _____
○ _____
○ _____
○ _____

Today I'm Grateful for

MINDFULNESS DAILY JOURNAL

MY DAY

10 MINUTES TO REFLECT ON YOUR DAY

3 Moments You'd Like To Remember

One Idea of Today That You'd Like To Explore Further

One of The Day's Challenges Big or Small

What I Did Wrong and How To Avoid That

MINDFULNESS DAILY JOURNAL

JOURNAL

goal

MINDFULNESS DAILY JOURNAL

Date: _____/_____/20__

Sun ○ Mon ○ Tue ○ Wed ○ Thu ○ Fri ○ Sat ○

IDEAS

MY MOOD TODAY

Today Will Be A Good Day

Meditation

How long? _____/_____   How was it?   Hard ○   Easy ○

Excercise ○   Yoga/Walking/Gym/Other _____

Today I Choose to Feel
_____
_____
_____

Today I Will Focus on
_____
_____
_____

Today I feel Inspired By
_____
_____
_____

Good Habits of The Day
_____
_____
_____

To Do List
○ _____
○ _____
○ _____
○ _____
○ _____
○ _____

Today I'm Grateful for

MINDFULNESS DAILY JOURNAL

MY DAY

10 MINUTES TO REFLECT ON YOUR DAY

3 Moments You'd Like To Remember

One Idea of Today That You'd Like To Explore Further

One of The Day's Challenges Big or Small

What I Did Wrong and How To Avoid That

MINDFULNESS DAILY JOURNAL

JOURNAL

goal

MINDFULNESS DAILY JOURNAL

Date: _____/_____/20__

Sun ○ Mon ○ Tue ○ Wed ○ Thu ○ Fri ○ Sat ○

IDEAS

MY MOOD TODAY

😊 ☹️ 😦 😄 😠

Today Will Be A Good Day

Meditation

How long? _____/_____   How was it? Hard ○   Easy ○

Excercise ○   Yoga/Walking/Gym/Other _____

Today I Choose to Feel

_____
_____
_____

Today I Will Focus on

_____
_____
_____

Today I feel Inspired By

_____
_____
_____

Good Habits of The Day

_____
_____
_____

To Do List

○ _____
○ _____
○ _____
○ _____
○ _____
○ _____

Today I'm Grateful for

MINDFULNESS DAILY JOURNAL

MY DAY

10 MINUTES TO REFLECT ON YOUR DAY

3 Moments You'd Like To Remember

One Idea of Today That You'd Like To Explore Further

One of The Day's Challenges Big or Small

What I Did Wrong and How To Avoid That

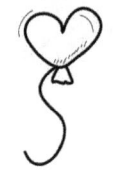

MINDFULNESS DAILY JOURNAL

JOURNAL

goal

MINDFULNESS DAILY JOURNAL

Date: _____/_____/20__

Sun ○ Mon ○ Tue ○ Wed ○ Thu ○ Fri ○ Sat ○

IDEAS

MY MOOD TODAY

☺ ☹ 😐 😄 😲

Today Will Be A Good Day

Meditation

How long? _____/_____   How was it?   Hard ○   Easy ○

Excercise ○   Yoga/Walking/Gym/Other _____

Today I Choose to Feel
_____
_____
_____

Today I Will Focus on
_____
_____
_____

Today I feel Inspired By
_____
_____
_____

Good Habits of The Day
_____
_____
_____

To Do List
○ _____
○ _____
○ _____
○ _____
○ _____

Today I'm Grateful for
_____
_____
_____
_____

MINDFULNESS DAILY JOURNAL

MY DAY

10 MINUTES TO REFLECT ON YOUR DAY

3 Moments You'd Like To Remember

One Idea of Today That You'd Like To Explore Further

One of The Day's Challenges Big or Small

What I Did Wrong and How To Avoid That

MINDFULNESS DAILY JOURNAL

JOURNAL

goal

MINDFULNESS DAILY JOURNAL

Date: _____/_____/20__

Sun ○ Mon ○ Tue ○ Wed ○ Thu ○ Fri ○ Sat ○

IDEAS

MY MOOD TODAY

😊 ☹️ 😦 😄 😠

Today will be a Good Day

Meditation

How long? _____/_____   How was it? Hard ○ Easy ○

Excercise ○   Yoga/Walking/Gym/Other _____

Today I Choose to Feel

_____
_____
_____

Today I Will Focus on

_____
_____
_____

Today I feel Inspired By

_____
_____
_____

Good Habits of The Day

_____
_____
_____

To Do List

○ _____
○ _____
○ _____
○ _____
○ _____
○ _____

Today I'm Grateful for

MINDFULNESS DAILY JOURNAL

MY DAY

10 MINUTES TO REFLECT ON YOUR DAY

3 Moments You'd Like To Remember

One Idea of Today That You'd Like To Explore Further

One of The Day's Challenges Big or Small

What I Did Wrong and How To Avoid That

MINDFULNESS DAILY JOURNAL

JOURNAL

goal

MINDFULNESS DAILY JOURNAL

Date: _____/_____/20__

Sun ◯   Mon ◯   Tue ◯   Wed ◯   Thu ◯   Fri ◯   Sat ◯

IDEAS

MY MOOD TODAY

😊 ☹️ 😐 😄 😠

Today Will Be A Good Day

Meditation

How long? _____ / _____   How was it?   Hard ◯   Easy ◯

Excercise ◯   Yoga/Walking/Gym/Other _____

Today I Choose to Feel
_____
_____
_____

Today I Will Focus on
_____
_____
_____

Today I feel Inspired By
_____
_____
_____

Good Habits of The Day
_____
_____
_____

To Do List
◯ _____
◯ _____
◯ _____
◯ _____
◯ _____
◯ _____

Today I'm Grateful for
_____
_____
_____

MINDFULNESS DAILY JOURNAL

MY DAY

10 MINUTES TO REFLECT ON YOUR DAY

3 Moments You'd Like To Remember

One Idea of Today That You'd Like To Explore Further

One of The Day's Challenges Big or Small

What I Did Wrong and How To Avoid That

MINDFULNESS DAILY JOURNAL

JOURNAL

goal

MINDFULNESS DAILY JOURNAL

Date: _____/_____/20___

Sun ○ Mon ○ Tue ○ Wed ○ Thu ○ Fri ○ Sat ○

IDEAS

MY MOOD TODAY

😊 ☹️ 😦 😄 😠

Today Will Be A Good Day

Meditation

How long? _____ / _____   How was it?   Hard ○   Easy ○

Excercise ○   Yoga/Walking/Gym/Other _____

Today I Choose to Feel

_____
_____
_____

Today I Will Focus on

_____
_____
_____

Today I feel Inspired By

_____
_____
_____

Good Habits of The Day

_____
_____
_____

To Do List

○ _____
○ _____
○ _____
○ _____
○ _____
○ _____

Today I'm Grateful for

GRATITUDE

MINDFULNESS DAILY JOURNAL

MY DAY

10 MINUTES TO REFLECT ON YOUR DAY

3 Moments You'd Like To Remember

One Idea of Today That You'd Like To Explore Further

One of The Day's Challenges Big or Small

What I Did Wrong and How To Avoid That

MINDFULNESS DAILY JOURNAL

JOURNAL

goal

MINDFULNESS DAILY JOURNAL

Date: _____/_____/20___

Sun ○ Mon ○ Tue ○ Wed ○ Thu ○ Fri ○ Sat ○

IDEAS

MY MOOD TODAY

Today Will Be A Good Day

Meditation

How long? _____/_____   How was it? Hard ○   Easy ○

Excercise ○   Yoga/Walking/Gym/Other _____

Today I Choose to Feel

_____
_____
_____

Today I Will Focus on

_____
_____
_____

Today I feel Inspired By

_____
_____
_____

Good Habits of The Day

_____
_____
_____

To Do List

○ _____
○ _____
○ _____
○ _____
○ _____

Today I'm Grateful for

MINDFULNESS DAILY JOURNAL

MY DAY

10 MINUTES TO REFLECT ON YOUR DAY

3 Moments You'd Like To Remember

One Idea of Today That You'd Like To Explore Further

One of The Day's Challenges Big or Small

What I Did Wrong and How To Avoid That

MINDFULNESS DAILY JOURNAL

JOURNAL

goal

MINDFULNESS DAILY JOURNAL

Date: _____/_____/20__

Sun ○   Mon ○   Tue ○   Wed ○   Thu ○   Fri ○   Sat ○

IDEAS

MY MOOD TODAY
🙂 ☹️ 😐 😄 😠

Today Will Be A Good Day

Meditation

How long? _____ / _____   How was it?   Hard ○   Easy ○

Excercise ○   Yoga/Walking/Gym/Other _____

Today I Choose to Feel

Today I Will Focus on

Today I feel Inspired By

Good Habits of The Day

To Do List

Today I'm Grateful for

MINDFULNESS DAILY JOURNAL

MY DAY

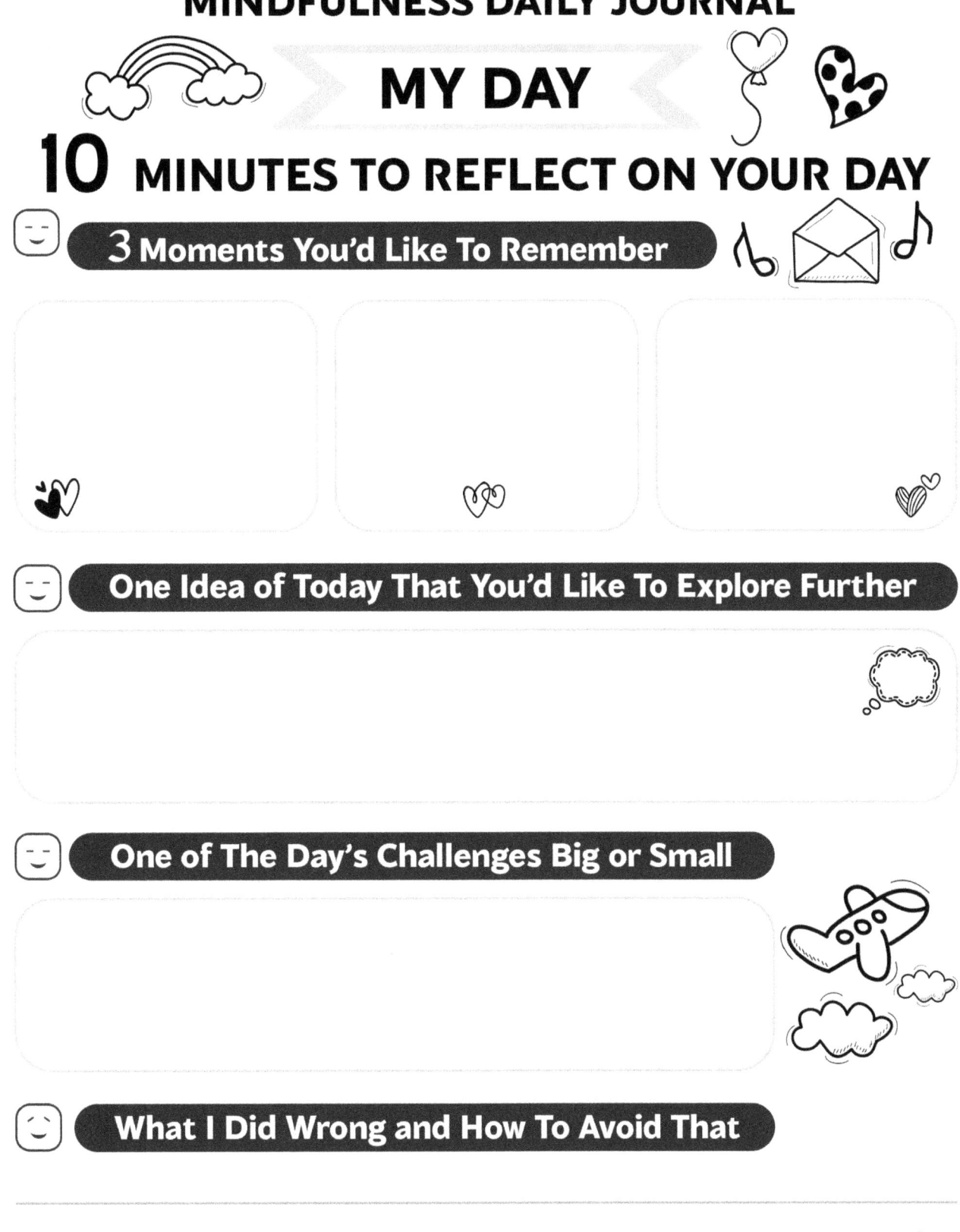

10 MINUTES TO REFLECT ON YOUR DAY

3 Moments You'd Like To Remember

One Idea of Today That You'd Like To Explore Further

One of The Day's Challenges Big or Small

What I Did Wrong and How To Avoid That

MINDFULNESS DAILY JOURNAL

JOURNAL

goal

MINDFULNESS DAILY JOURNAL

Date: ____/____/20__

Sun ◯ Mon ◯ Tue ◯ Wed ◯ Thu ◯ Fri ◯ Sat ◯

IDEAS

MY MOOD TODAY

😊 ☹️ 😐 😄 😠

Today Will Be A Good Day

Meditation

How long? ____/____

How was it? Hard ◯ Easy ◯

Exercise ◯   Yoga/Walking/Gym/Other _____

Today I Choose to Feel
_____
_____
_____

Today I Will Focus on
_____
_____
_____

Today I feel Inspired By
_____
_____
_____

Good Habits of The Day
_____
_____
_____

To Do List
◯ _____
◯ _____
◯ _____
◯ _____
◯ _____
◯ _____

Today I'm Grateful for

MINDFULNESS DAILY JOURNAL

MY DAY

10 MINUTES TO REFLECT ON YOUR DAY

3 Moments You'd Like To Remember

One Idea of Today That You'd Like To Explore Further

One of The Day's Challenges Big or Small

What I Did Wrong and How To Avoid That

MINDFULNESS DAILY JOURNAL

JOURNAL

goal

MINDFULNESS DAILY JOURNAL

Date: _____/_____/20___

Sun ◯ Mon ◯ Tue ◯ Wed ◯ Thu ◯ Fri ◯ Sat ◯

IDEAS

MY MOOD TODAY
🙂 ☹️ 😦 😄 😠

Today Will Be A Good Day

Meditation

How long? _____ / _____   How was it? Hard ◯   Easy ◯

Excercise ◯   Yoga/Walking/Gym/Other _____

Today I Choose to Feel

_____
_____
_____

Today I Will Focus on

_____
_____
_____

Today I feel Inspired By

_____
_____
_____

Good Habits of The Day

_____
_____
_____

To Do List

◯ _____
◯ _____
◯ _____
◯ _____
◯ _____
◯ _____

Today I'm Grateful for

GRATITUDE

MINDFULNESS DAILY JOURNAL

MY DAY

10 MINUTES TO REFLECT ON YOUR DAY

3 Moments You'd Like To Remember

One Idea of Today That You'd Like To Explore Further

One of The Day's Challenges Big or Small

What I Did Wrong and How To Avoid That

MINDFULNESS DAILY JOURNAL

JOURNAL

goal

MINDFULNESS DAILY JOURNAL

Date: _____/_____/20__

Sun ○   Mon ○   Tue ○   Wed ○   Thu ○   Fri ○   Sat ○

IDEAS

MY MOOD TODAY

😊 ☹️ 😖 😄 😠

Today Will Be A Good Day

Meditation

How long? _____ /_____

How was it?   Hard ○   Easy ○

Excercise ○   Yoga/Walking/Gym/Other _____

Today I Choose to Feel
_____
_____
_____

Today I Will Focus on
_____
_____
_____

Today I feel Inspired By
_____
_____
_____

Good Habits of The Day
_____
_____
_____

To Do List
☐ _____
☐ _____
☐ _____
☐ _____
☐ _____

Today I'm Grateful for

MINDFULNESS DAILY JOURNAL

MY DAY

10 MINUTES TO REFLECT ON YOUR DAY

3 Moments You'd Like To Remember

One Idea of Today That You'd Like To Explore Further

One of The Day's Challenges Big or Small

What I Did Wrong and How To Avoid That

MINDFULNESS DAILY JOURNAL

JOURNAL

goal

MINDFULNESS DAILY JOURNAL

Date: _____/_____/20__

Sun ○ Mon ○ Tue ○ Wed ○ Thu ○ Fri ○ Sat ○

IDEAS

MY MOOD TODAY
☺ ☹ ☹ 😄 😠

Today will be a Good Day

Meditation

How long? _____ / _____   How was it?   Hard ○   Easy ○

Excercise ○   Yoga/Walking/Gym/Other _____

Today I Choose to Feel

Today I Will Focus on

Today I feel Inspired By

Good Habits of The Day

To Do List

Today I'm Grateful for

MINDFULNESS DAILY JOURNAL

MY DAY

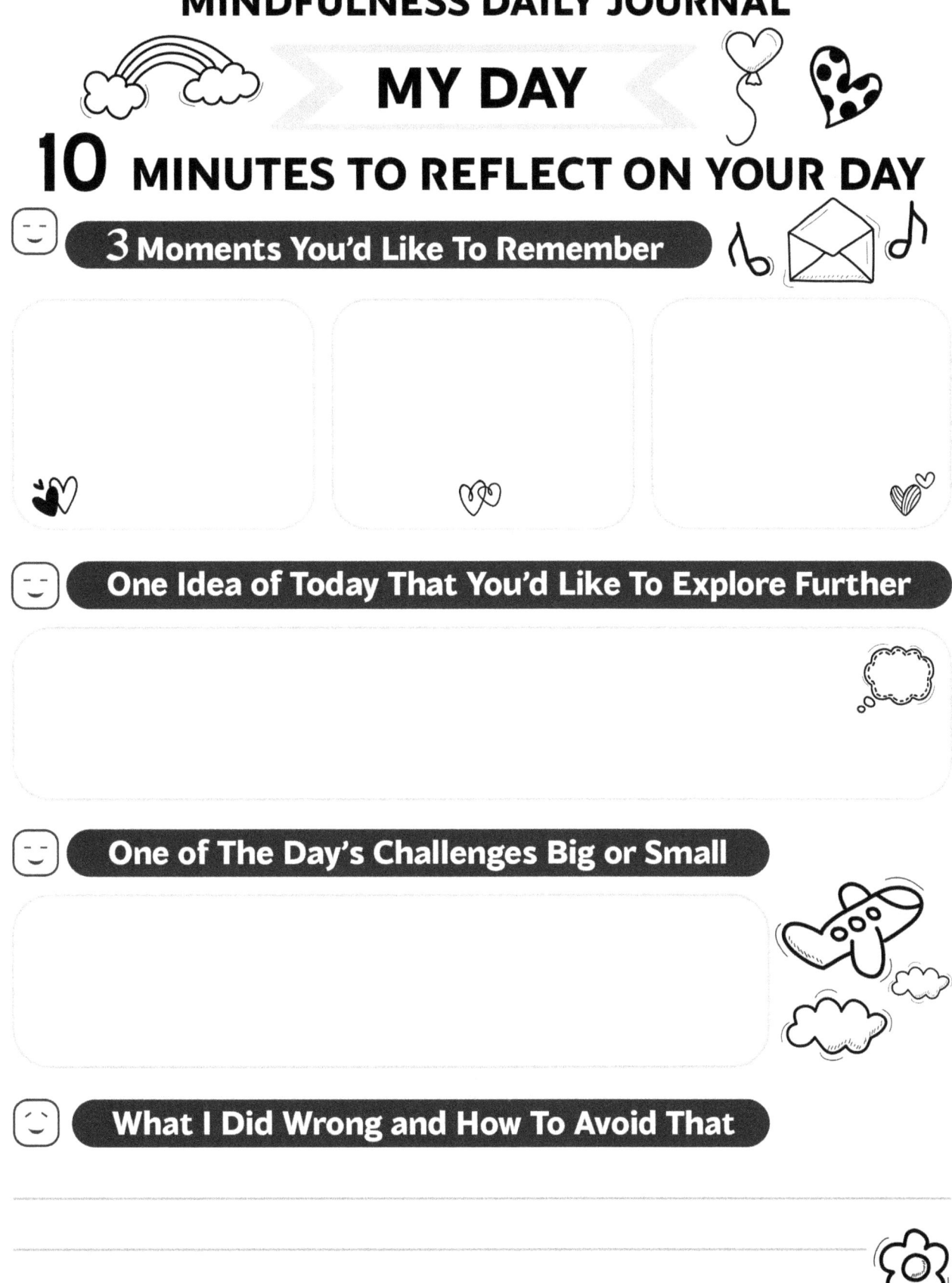

10 MINUTES TO REFLECT ON YOUR DAY

3 Moments You'd Like To Remember

One Idea of Today That You'd Like To Explore Further

One of The Day's Challenges Big or Small

What I Did Wrong and How To Avoid That

MINDFULNESS DAILY JOURNAL

JOURNAL

goal

MINDFULNESS DAILY JOURNAL

Date: _____/_____/20__

Sun ○ Mon ○ Tue ○ Wed ○ Thu ○ Fri ○ Sat ○

IDEAS

MY MOOD TODAY

🙂 🙁 😦 😄 😠

Today Will Be A Good Day

Meditation

How long? _____ / _____

How was it? Hard ○ Easy ○

Excercise ○   Yoga/Walking/Gym/Other _____

Today I Choose to Feel
_____
_____
_____

Today I Will Focus on
_____
_____
_____

Today I feel Inspired By
_____
_____
_____

Good Habits of The Day
_____
_____
_____

To Do List
☐ _____
☐ _____
☐ _____
☐ _____
☐ _____
☐ _____

Today I'm Grateful for

MINDFULNESS DAILY JOURNAL

MY DAY

10 MINUTES TO REFLECT ON YOUR DAY

3 Moments You'd Like To Remember

One Idea of Today That You'd Like To Explore Further

One of The Day's Challenges Big or Small

What I Did Wrong and How To Avoid That

MINDFULNESS DAILY JOURNAL

JOURNAL

goal

MINDFULNESS DAILY JOURNAL

Date: _____/_____/20__

Sun ○ Mon ○ Tue ○ Wed ○ Thu ○ Fri ○ Sat ○

IDEAS

MY MOOD TODAY

☺ ☹ 😐 😄 😠

Today Will Be A Good Day

Meditation

How long? _____ / _____

How was it? Hard ○ Easy ○

Excercise ○   Yoga/Walking/Gym/Other _____

Today I Choose to Feel
_____
_____
_____

Today I Will Focus on
_____
_____
_____

Today I feel Inspired By
_____
_____
_____

Good Habits of The Day
_____
_____
_____

To Do List
○ _____
○ _____
○ _____
○ _____
○ _____
○ _____

Today I'm Grateful for

GRATITUDE

MINDFULNESS DAILY JOURNAL

MY DAY

10 MINUTES TO REFLECT ON YOUR DAY

3 Moments You'd Like To Remember

One Idea of Today That You'd Like To Explore Further

One of The Day's Challenges Big or Small

What I Did Wrong and How To Avoid That

MINDFULNESS DAILY JOURNAL

JOURNAL

goal

MINDFULNESS DAILY JOURNAL

Date: _____/_____/20__

Sun ○ Mon ○ Tue ○ Wed ○ Thu ○ Fri ○ Sat ○

IDEAS

MY MOOD TODAY
☺ ☹ ☹ 😄 😠

Today Will Be A Good Day

Meditation

How long? _____ / _____   How was it?   Hard ○   Easy ○

Exercise ○   Yoga/Walking/Gym/Other _____

Today I Choose to Feel
_____
_____
_____

Today I Will Focus on
_____
_____
_____

Today I feel Inspired By
_____
_____
_____

Good Habits of The Day
_____
_____
_____

To Do List
○ _____
○ _____
○ _____
○ _____
○ _____
○ _____

Today I'm Grateful for

MINDFULNESS DAILY JOURNAL

MY DAY

10 MINUTES TO REFLECT ON YOUR DAY

3 Moments You'd Like To Remember

One Idea of Today That You'd Like To Explore Further

One of The Day's Challenges Big or Small

What I Did Wrong and How To Avoid That

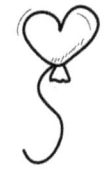

MINDFULNESS DAILY JOURNAL

JOURNAL

goal

MINDFULNESS DAILY JOURNAL

Date: _____/_____/20__

Sun ○   Mon ○   Tue ○   Wed ○   Thu ○   Fri ○   Sat ○

IDEAS

MY MOOD TODAY

😊 ☹️ 😐 😄 😮

Today Will Be A Good Day

Meditation

How long? _____/_____   How was it?   Hard ○   Easy ○

Excercise ○   Yoga/Walking/Gym/Other _____

Today I Choose to Feel
_____
_____
_____

Today I Will Focus on
_____
_____
_____

Today I feel Inspired By
_____
_____
_____

Good Habits of The Day
_____
_____
_____

To Do List
○ _____
○ _____
○ _____
○ _____
○ _____
○ _____

Today I'm Grateful for

MINDFULNESS DAILY JOURNAL

MY DAY

10 MINUTES TO REFLECT ON YOUR DAY

3 Moments You'd Like To Remember

One Idea of Today That You'd Like To Explore Further

One of The Day's Challenges Big or Small

What I Did Wrong and How To Avoid That

MINDFULNESS DAILY JOURNAL

JOURNAL

goal

MINDFULNESS DAILY JOURNAL

Date: _____/_____/20__

Sun ○ Mon ○ Tue ○ Wed ○ Thu ○ Fri ○ Sat ○

IDEAS

MY MOOD TODAY

Today Will Be A Good Day

Meditation

How long? _____ / _____   How was it?   Hard ○   Easy ○

Excercise ○   Yoga/Walking/Gym/Other _____

Today I Choose to Feel

Today I Will Focus on

Today I feel Inspired By

Good Habits of The Day

To Do List

Today I'm Grateful for

MINDFULNESS DAILY JOURNAL

MY DAY

10 MINUTES TO REFLECT ON YOUR DAY

3 Moments You'd Like To Remember

One Idea of Today That You'd Like To Explore Further

One of The Day's Challenges Big or Small

What I Did Wrong and How To Avoid That

MINDFULNESS DAILY JOURNAL

JOURNAL

goal

MINDFULNESS DAILY JOURNAL

Date: _____/_____/20__

Sun Mon Tue Wed Thu Fri Sat

IDEAS

MY MOOD TODAY

Today Will Be A Good Day

Meditation

How long? _____ / _____   How was it?   Hard ◯   Easy ◯

Excercise ◯   Yoga/Walking/Gym/Other _____

Today I Choose to Feel

_____
_____
_____
_____

Today I Will Focus on

_____
_____
_____
_____

Today I feel Inspired By

_____
_____
_____
_____

Good Habits of The Day

_____
_____
_____
_____

To Do List

◯ _____
◯ _____
◯ _____
◯ _____
◯ _____
◯ _____

Today I'm Grateful for

MINDFULNESS DAILY JOURNAL

MY DAY

10 MINUTES TO REFLECT ON YOUR DAY

3 Moments You'd Like To Remember

One Idea of Today That You'd Like To Explore Further

One of The Day's Challenges Big or Small

What I Did Wrong and How To Avoid That

MINDFULNESS DAILY JOURNAL

JOURNAL

goal

MINDFULNESS DAILY JOURNAL

Date: _____/_____/20___

Sun ○ Mon ○ Tue ○ Wed ○ Thu ○ Fri ○ Sat ○

IDEAS

MY MOOD TODAY

🙂 ☹️ 😐 😄 😲

Today Will Be A Good Day

Meditation

How long? _____/_____   How was it?   Hard ○   Easy ○

Exercise ○   Yoga/Walking/Gym/Other _____

Today I Choose to Feel
_____
_____
_____

Today I Will Focus on
_____
_____
_____

Today I feel Inspired By
_____
_____
_____

Good Habits of The Day
_____
_____
_____

To Do List

- _____
- _____
- _____
- _____
- _____

Today I'm Grateful for
_____
_____
_____

MINDFULNESS DAILY JOURNAL

MY DAY

10 MINUTES TO REFLECT ON YOUR DAY

3 Moments You'd Like To Remember

One Idea of Today That You'd Like To Explore Further

One of The Day's Challenges Big or Small

What I Did Wrong and How To Avoid That

MINDFULNESS DAILY JOURNAL

JOURNAL

goal

MINDFULNESS DAILY JOURNAL

Date: _____/_____/20__

Sun ○ Mon ○ Tue ○ Wed ○ Thu ○ Fri ○ Sat ○

IDEAS

MY MOOD TODAY

😊 ☹ 😦 😄 😠

Today Will Be A Good Day

Meditation

How long? _____ / _____

How was it? Hard ○ Easy ○

Excercise ○ Yoga/Walking/Gym/Other _____

Today I Choose to Feel
_____
_____
_____

Today I Will Focus on
_____
_____
_____

Today I feel Inspired By
_____
_____
_____

Good Habits of The Day
_____
_____
_____

To Do List
○ _____
○ _____
○ _____
○ _____
○ _____
○ _____

Today I'm Grateful for
_____
_____
_____
_____

MINDFULNESS DAILY JOURNAL

JOURNAL

goal

MINDFULNESS DAILY JOURNAL

Date: _____/_____/20__

Sun ○ Mon ○ Tue ○ Wed ○ Thu ○ Fri ○ Sat ○

IDEAS

MY MOOD TODAY
😊 ☹️ 😣 😄 😮

Today Will Be A Good Day

Meditation

How long? _____ /_____   How was it?   Hard ○   Easy ○

Excercise ○   Yoga/Walking/Gym/Other _____

Today I Choose to Feel
_____
_____
_____

Today I Will Focus on
_____
_____
_____

Today I feel Inspired By
_____
_____
_____

Good Habits of The Day
_____
_____
_____

To Do List
○ _____
○ _____
○ _____
○ _____
○ _____
○ _____

Today I'm Grateful for
_____
_____
_____
_____

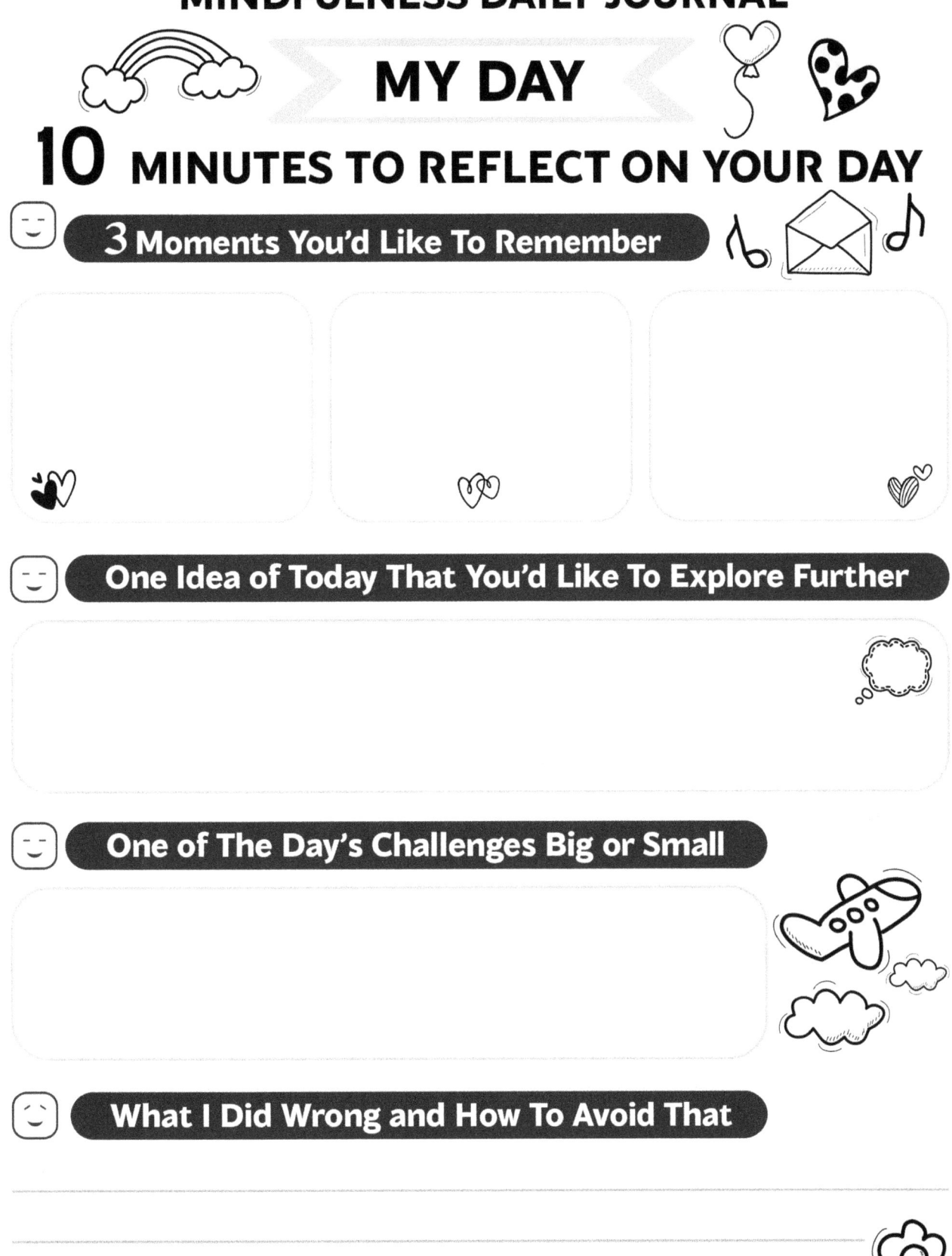

MINDFULNESS DAILY JOURNAL

MY DAY

10 MINUTES TO REFLECT ON YOUR DAY

3 Moments You'd Like To Remember

One Idea of Today That You'd Like To Explore Further

One of The Day's Challenges Big or Small

What I Did Wrong and How To Avoid That

MINDFULNESS DAILY JOURNAL

JOURNAL

goal

MINDFULNESS DAILY JOURNAL

Date: _____/_____/20__

Sun ○ Mon ○ Tue ○ Wed ○ Thu ○ Fri ○ Sat ○

IDEAS

MY MOOD TODAY

☺ ☹ 😐 😄 😠

Today Will Be A Good Day

Meditation

How long? _____ / _____   How was it?   Hard ○   Easy ○

Excercise ○   Yoga/Walking/Gym/Other _____

Today I Choose to Feel
_____
_____
_____

Today I Will Focus on
_____
_____
_____

Today I feel Inspired By
_____
_____
_____

Good Habits of The Day
_____
_____
_____

To Do List
○ _____
○ _____
○ _____
○ _____
○ _____
○ _____

Today I'm Grateful for

GRATITUDE

MINDFULNESS DAILY JOURNAL

MY DAY

10 MINUTES TO REFLECT ON YOUR DAY

3 Moments You'd Like To Remember

One Idea of Today That You'd Like To Explore Further

One of The Day's Challenges Big or Small

What I Did Wrong and How To Avoid That

MINDFULNESS DAILY JOURNAL

JOURNAL

goal

Journal

MINDFULNESS DAILY JOURNAL

JOURNAL

goal

MINDFULNESS DAILY JOURNAL

JOURNAL

goal

MINDFULNESS DAILY JOURNAL

JOURNAL

goal

MINDFULNESS DAILY JOURNAL

JOURNAL

goal

MINDFULNESS DAILY JOURNAL

JOURNAL

goal

MINDFULNESS DAILY JOURNAL

JOURNAL

goal

MINDFULNESS DAILY JOURNAL

JOURNAL

goal

MINDFULNESS DAILY JOURNAL

JOURNAL

goal

MINDFULNESS DAILY JOURNAL

JOURNAL

goal

MINDFULNESS DAILY JOURNAL

JOURNAL

goal

MINDFULNESS DAILY JOURNAL

JOURNAL

goal

MINDFULNESS DAILY JOURNAL

JOURNAL

goal

MINDFULNESS DAILY JOURNAL

JOURNAL

goal

MINDFULNESS DAILY JOURNAL

JOURNAL

goal

MINDFULNESS DAILY JOURNAL

JOURNAL

goal

MINDFULNESS DAILY JOURNAL

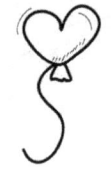

JOURNAL

goal

MINDFULNESS DAILY JOURNAL

JOURNAL

goal

MINDFULNESS DAILY JOURNAL

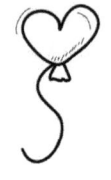

JOURNAL

goal

MINDFULNESS DAILY JOURNAL

JOURNAL

goal

MINDFULNESS DAILY JOURNAL

JOURNAL

goal

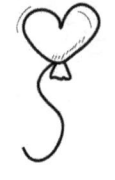

MINDFULNESS DAILY JOURNAL

JOURNAL

goal

MINDFULNESS DAILY JOURNAL

JOURNAL

goal

MINDFULNESS DAILY JOURNAL

JOURNAL

goal

MINDFULNESS DAILY JOURNAL

JOURNAL

goal

MINDFULNESS DAILY JOURNAL

JOURNAL

goal

MINDFULNESS DAILY JOURNAL

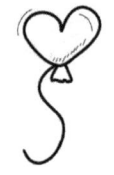

JOURNAL

goal

MINDFULNESS DAILY JOURNAL

JOURNAL

goal

MINDFULNESS DAILY JOURNAL

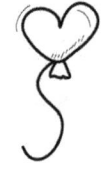

JOURNAL

goal

MINDFULNESS DAILY JOURNAL

JOURNAL

goal

MINDFULNESS DAILY JOURNAL

JOURNAL

goal

Printed in the USA
CPSIA information can be obtained
at www.ICGtesting.com
LVHW060210050424
776522LV00022B/337